EXPLORER BOOKS

BATS

by
Lisa deMauro

Sincere thanks to
Bat Conservation International, Inc.
for its valuable help.

Published by The Trumpet Club
a division of Bantam Doubleday Dell Publishing Group, Inc.
666 Fifth Avenue, New York, New York 10103

ISBN: 0-440-84218-2

Produced by Parachute Press, Inc.
Printed in the United States of America
March 1990

10 9 8 7 6 5 4 3 2 1
CW

Photographs by Merlin D. Tuttle, Bat Conservation International, Inc.

Contents

Introduction

Ready or not, you're about to plunge into a world of darkness. Night is falling in the forest. The last glow of daylight is slipping away. Colors seem to be fading. All around you, gray and black shapes are looming. You can hardly tell where one shadowy tree ends and another begins. The ground is uneven. You stumble.

And then you stop and listen.

It's dark, but it's not quiet. The night is filled with sounds. There are rasping, whirring noises in the air. Leaves crinkle and bushes rustle. Suddenly a branch snaps behind you. Your heart begins to pound.

You realize that you are not alone. There are living creatures in this forest. They're all around you, slithering, scuttling, and darting through the darkness.

Something moves against the sky. Is it a bird? More figures appear, swooping back and forth. But wait. Those aren't birds. They're bats! Lots of them! Yikes!

Is this giving you the creeps? You're in good company. Ever since people first walked the earth, they have been afraid of the night and of the animals that are at home in the darkness.

The reason is simple enough: People are creatures of the daylight. Our eyes are well-suited to see color and detail. But for that we need light. As the light fades, so does the sharpness of our vision. The darker it gets, the less we can see.

People with normal vision depend more on their eyes than on any other sense for finding their way in the world. In the dark, as our sight becomes weaker, we begin to feel lost and defenseless. And when we discover animals that move easily and see well in the dark, we feel even more uncomfortable.

People who lived long ago imagined that nocturnal animals—those that were active at night and rested by day—were up to no good. The people thought that if any creature moved about only at night, then it must have something to hide. Otherwise, it would come out in the daylight, like everyone else. Since these creatures could see in the dark, they could attack without warning and escape without harm, so the people decided that these night animals were probably dangerous, too.

Of course, things have changed. Nowadays, we can often control the darkness around us. We can light up the night with street lamps and headlights. And for those late-night walks in the woods, we have lanterns and flashlights to show us the way.

Most of us no longer fear the night the way some of our ancestors did. And yet, there is something about the night that still makes many of us uncomfortable. We can't help but wonder *why* any animal would turn away from the daylight and do all its active living at night. In this book, you'll learn some of the reasons why.

1

Creatures of the Night

Picture this: Somehow your "inner clock" gets set twelve hours ahead. Everyone else in your family is yawning and heading for bed but not you. You're wide awake. You eat a bowl of corn-flakes and then settle in for a long night. You read, reorganize your record collection, and play some cards. Then you do some exercises, write a few letters, and sit down for a big dinner. Finally, at the first light of dawn, you crawl into bed and sleep deeply. Then when the sun goes down, it all begins again. You come to life at night. By day, you rest.

If you suddenly became nocturnal, it would probably be because something about you had changed—*a lot!* To find out what that might be, you'd want to look at creatures that are naturally nocturnal. What traits make these creatures well suited to a nocturnal life? Why would an animal be nocturnal when it seems so much easier to be active by day?

Some of the answers are found in better physical conditions, greater safety, or a bigger food supply.

The Physical Conditions

There are exceptions to almost every rule in nature and that holds true for the nocturnal world. Many night creatures are not strictly nocturnal. Some, for example, come out during the day when conditions are right. The garden slug is that type of nocturnal animal.

Slugs are snails without the shell. They're slimy and soft. Their bodies are covered with slippery mucus. And they come creeping out at night, often to chew on the flowers and vegetables that people plant in their gardens.

Why are they nocturnal? Slugs do not have layers of skin cells to protect them the way people and many other animals do. In weather that is very warm or very dry, they begin to dry out. If they lose too much body fluid, they die. For that reason, they have to wait for night to bring cooler temperatures and moister air. Then they creep out from their hiding places in the soil, under stones, or beneath fallen trees. They feed on plants or dead leaves. But they don't always return to their homes promptly at dawn. On cool, rainy mornings, when the temperature stays low, slugs keep feeding after sunrise.

Some types of slugs can be a problem for gardeners. But other types feed mostly on decaying plants and leaves. They help make new, rich soil out of the food they eat. And research on slug mucus may help answer important questions about some human diseases.

A hippopotamus may seem like a far cry from a garden slug. But hippos are another type of animal that is more active when the sun goes down. Unlike slugs, hippos have a thick hide—as much as an inch and a half thick in some places. But a hippo also loses water easily through its skin.

For this reason, hippos usually spend their days swimming or wading in the water, with only their noses, eyes, and ears above the surface. Sometimes they come out for a short sunbath. Then they return to the water until sundown. At that point, they head for the banks to graze on the grass, eating about 500 pounds of grass each night!

Desert and Forest Creatures

Moisture-loving animals like the slug and hippo could never live in a desert where hot dry air meets hot dry earth. To survive in the desert, an animal must get by on very little water. And it must find ways to keep from overheating and drying out.

Most desert animals lie low when the sun is at its worst. They burrow into the cooler, moister ground by day. Then at night, temperatures drop fast and the search for food begins.

The pit viper is a poisonous snake, which keeps cool in the shade during daylight hours and becomes active at night. This animal has a special trait that makes it a very successful night hunter. Behind its nostrils are two sensory pits that react to temperature. The snake can sense the heat that is given off by the body of an animal. This way, it can find its food in the dark. The rattlesnake is one of the more common pit vipers. Their bites are dangerous to people as well as to the animals they hunt.

Desert creatures have other reasons for being nocturnal. The small amount of moisture that is in the desert air turns to dew on desert plants at night. Animals that feed on these plants at night get a bonus drink with their meal! And those that feed on other animals, rather than on plants, find better hunting at night. The daylight hours are too hot for most of the prey, so they come out at night.

Animals of the forest have less to fear from the burning rays of the sun. But they have their own reasons for being nocturnal. For the slender loris of southern India and Sri Lanka, being a night creature makes it easier to catch food. This small, furry animal, a relative of the monkey, has a rounded head, rounded ears and huge round eyes that provide it with excellent night vision.

By day, the slender loris sleeps in the trees. After dark, it moves very slowly through the branches, looking for lizards and insects, or small birds in nests.

Night Owls and Alley Cats

Most owls are nocturnal. They fly by night and sleep by day. There are some owls that are active during the day, but most are not because they are best suited for night hunting. Their usual prey consists of rodents, snakes, birds, lizards, and some bats. Owls hunt in daylight only in areas where there are no hawks or other day-hunting birds. In other words, the hunting is best when there is no competition.

The eyes of an owl are very big. That means they can gather a lot of light—a feature that is very important for good night vision. Owl eyes are shaped like tubes rather than balls. Because of their shape and size, the eyes can't roll from side to side or top to bottom. But owls can turn their heads around until they are facing backward. They can also turn their heads almost completely upside down. So they can see what's going on all around them.

Owls also have excellent hearing. (But don't confuse the tufts of feathers which you can see on some owls with ears. All owls have ears that are hidden under their feathers.) Owls can see very well at night. But when there is very little light, or none at all, owls can track their prey by sound. They have another secret weapon: silent flight. Around the edges of an owl's wings are small fringes. These fringes muffle the sound of the flapping wings as the owl flies toward its prey. This way, the bird can strike without warning.

You may not think of cats as nocturnal animals, but they are. (Cats are known for disturbing the night peace with their meowing. In cartoons they often get shoes thrown at them for making their midnight racket!)

Although they're often active by day, cats have the equipment to function in the dark, too. There's a special layer in a cat's eye called a *tapetum*. This layer catches light and reflects it back into the eye. This lets the cat make the most of very dim light. The tapetum is what causes the "eyeshine" you see when a cat steps into the path of a bright light at night. (Foxes, deer, and some other nocturnal animals have a tapetum, too.)

Cats have a long and confusing history. People began keeping cats as pets about 5,000 years ago.

In ancient Egypt, there were cat goddesses. In ancient Thailand, cats were thought to carry the souls of holy men. In Europe during the Middle Ages, cats got a reputation for bad luck—especially black cats. People thought they were witches in disguise, or agents of the devil.

Today, cats are a popular household pet. Nowadays when people think of a night animal that is frightening or evil, it isn't cats they think of. It's bats!

Creatures of the Night Sky

Bats are perhaps the most nocturnal of animals. While many night creatures have some active days, bats tend to remain active only at night.

Why? Let's first take a look at the kind of bats that eat insects. As you will learn later on, they have a special system of catching insects, which gives them a huge advantage over other night hunters. For that reason, no animal is better suited for the night shift. Insect-eating bats find a wide selection of night-flying insects. And they have to share their findings with very few other animals. If bats were to look for food by day, they would be competing for the insect supply with a large number of birds.

In addition, bats are much safer under the blanket of darkness. By day, they would be easy prey for hunting birds that like to eat bats, such as the bat hawk and the bat falcon. Bats face the most danger just after sunset while there is still some light in the sky. Clearly, bats would be caught more easily if they were all out flying in broad daylight.

Some bats eat fruit and nectar. These bats have good reason to be nocturnal, as well. By day, they would have to compete for their food with birds that shared their diet. By feeding at night, bats have their pick of the fruits and of "bat" flowers that blossom only at night. Even more importantly, nighttime offers these bats protection from many predators.

But even bats can develop unexpected behavior when conditions are right. When there are no hunting birds around, bats may even shed some of their nocturnal habits. On some Pacific islands, where there are no predators to bother them, bats are active by day at least part of the time. On Samoa, there are bats that seem never to be nocturnal, but these are unusual. The great majority of bats are only active at night.

In the chapters that follow, you'll get a closer look at the bat. And when you reach the end of this book, you'll know many of the secrets of this most famous of all night creatures.

2

Meet the Bats

For thousands of years, people thought bats were evil spirits who could work spells. We may not believe in evil spirits anymore, but people still behave as though they're under a strange spell when they are around bats. Here's what can happen:

Begin with one person. It can be a friendly, brave person. It can even be someone who usually loves animals.

Now take one bat. Make it a shy bat. (Bats tend to be shy.) Make it a small bat. (One of the more common North American bats, the little brown bat, may weigh less than ¼ ounce—about the same as seven paper clips.) Make it a bat that doesn't like to bite people. (Bats have very little interest in biting people.)

Now put the person and the bat into the same room and watch what happens....

In no time at all the friendly, brave animal-lover will turn into a terrified, shrieking bat-hater, looking for a broom or a tennis racket to use in "self-defense."

Most people would never kick a stray cat or swat at a lost bird. But let a bat take a wrong turn into their living room and watch out! Why do people behave this way? Probably because so many people have so many wrong ideas about bats.

Here are ten things that many people (and maybe you) have heard about bats that are *not* true!

1. Bats are rodents. They're like mice with wings.

False. Bats are not rodents. In fact, they're most closely related to primates. That group includes monkeys, apes, and humans.

2. Bats are blind.

False. All bats can see. Some bats have very good night vision and rely on their eyes to find food.

3. Bats are dirty.

False. Bats are very clean animals. They spend much of their time grooming themselves, twisting and turning to get at hard-to-reach spots.

4. Bats commonly infect people with diseases, especially rabies.

False. Like dogs, raccoons, and people, bats can catch rabies. But they rarely pass on the disease (or any disease) to people. Fewer than twenty people in North America have died of any bat-related disease in the last forty years!

5. Bats like to attack people. They'll swoop at you and bite.

False. Bats are not aggressive—except toward their prey. (In North America, that almost always means insects.) People, on the other hand, frequently attack and destroy bats for no good reason at all.

6. Bats often get tangled in human hair.

False. Many scientists have experimented with bats to see if they would become tangled in human hair. They wouldn't.

7. Most bats drink blood.

False. Vampire bats drink blood—and vampires are rare. There are just three species of vampire out of nearly 1,000 species of bat. Most bats eat insects, fruit, or nectar.

8. Bats are useless pests.

False. Bats are *very* important to humans. Bats that feed on insects eat huge amounts of them every day. Just one small bat in your backyard can catch 600 mosquitoes in *one hour*! Bats that eat fruit and nectar spread seeds and help flowers grow. Without bats many important plants would not thrive.

9. There are plenty of bats in the world. We don't have to worry about them dying out.

False. There *are* a lot of bats in the world, but their numbers are shrinking. Some types are already extinct. The biggest reason is people. Some bats are killed outright by people who fear them or believe they cause trouble. Some are killed by hunters who sell the bats for their meat. Many bats die when people explore their caves and disturb their winter-long sleep. Sometimes these explorers interrupt the mother bats who are caring for their young. Most females give birth to only one baby a year, and that baby can't reproduce for about a year. So it takes a long time to build up a bat population. (It's a lot different for rodents. One pair of mice can produce fifty babies in a year, and each baby can begin reproducing five or six weeks after birth.)

10. Bats drive people crazy. That's where the expression "you have bats in your belfry" comes from.

False. Bats don't drive people insane. But, once you get to know bats, you might like them so much they'll make you batty!

If bats are such good guys, why doesn't anybody like them? Actually, in some parts of the world, people do like bats. In ancient Chinese art, for example, bats were often used to represent good fortune. Parts of Asia, Africa, Australia, and some islands in the Pacific Ocean are home to the bats known as flying foxes. (They get their name from the way they look; many have fox-like faces.) The biggest bats on earth are a type of flying fox.

Most flying foxes spend their days hanging from high branches out in the open. People are used to seeing them. They don't think the flying foxes are terrifying or mysterious. In fact, they are sometimes thought to bring good luck. (They are also used as food by many people.)

But the bats in Europe and North America are different. They're hard to get to know. They hide away in caves or musty buildings during the day. And then at night, when they're busy getting food, they're almost impossible to follow. They're small and quick. They dart and swoop at insects that we can't even see. They're shy, too.

Then there's the problem of how they look. Hanging from a rafter, wrapped in leathery wings, they're very different from our usual ideas of cuddly and cute. And their faces are not very attractive, to say the least!

Many of the bats in this part of the world have strange-shaped noses with pieces of flesh on them that look like spears. Some have folds of skin or fleshy horseshoe shapes on their faces. Many have ears that stick out. As you'll see in this book, bats look the way they do for a very good reason. The spears, folds, and big ears help them find their way to their food. But these features, to human eyes, can be scary-looking because of our superstitions. Some of them look like old pictures of demons.

Years ago, some people thought bats *were* demons, or witches. In Europe, many bats—and some people with the bad luck to have bats in their attics—were killed.

The Physical Facts

A bat's anatomy, or physical makeup, some-times leaves people wondering where exactly the bat fits in the animal kingdom. Is it a bird? Is it a rodent? Is it a mammal? Bats were the subject of several tales by the ancient Greek storyteller, Aesop. His stories pointed out how confused everyone was about bats.

In one story, the birds and the beasts have a war. At first the bats say that they are mice so that they can fight on the side of the beasts. Then they claim to be birds and they fight against the beasts. They switch from one side to the other, depending on who is winning. Finally, the other animals see what is going on and be-come angry. Both sides decide that they don't want the bats. By this time, the bats are so mixed up, they don't know *what* they are. They just fly off into the night, alone and ashamed.

Thousands of years ago, bats were thought to be a type of bird. More recently, they have been called flying mice. (The German word for bat, *fleder-maus,* means flying mouse; in Spanish, the words for bats—*ratones voladores*—mean *flying mice.*)

Bats do have some things in common with mice. Many are the size of a mouse. Some have tails that look like a mouse's. Some have mouse-like ears. And, like mice, they are mammals—they make up the second largest group of mam-mals! That means they have fur on their bodies (which may be brown, black, gray, reddish, orange, yellow, tan, spotted, or frosted with white); their babies are born alive, rather than hatched from eggs; and the mother produces milk to feed her newborn.

But unlike mice, or any other mammal, bats can fly. Some mammals, such as flying squirrels, have skin flaps that let them glide when they leap from a high branch. But that is not the same as *really* flying. Bats are the only mammals that can truly fly, using wings to power their flight and move in any direction they choose.

It is a bat's wings that give it its scientific name. Bats belong to an order known by experts as *Chiroptera* (ker-OP-ter-a). The name means "hand wing" and if you look closely at a bat's wing, you'll see how well the name fits. The bones of the wing are made up of a short upper arm, a long forearm, and then the hand: four long fingers and a short thumb. At the end of the thumb is a hook-like claw.

Bat wings are made up of a double layer of skin, called a membrane. The membrane is full of muscles so it is stretchy and puckered. When a bat spreads its wings, the membrane pulls tightly across the bones. When the wings are folded, the membrane snaps back, like a piece of elastic. It doesn't hang loosely. Bats keep their wings and their fur well groomed. They lick every inch of their wings, and wet their claws to reach out-of-the-way spots.

Some bats have another section of membrane

that connects their legs and tail. If a bat's tail is short, it may be completely covered by the membrane. In some bats, the tail is longer and sticks out from the membrane. Different bats use their tails and tail membrane in different ways: to help change directions in flight; as a basket for carrying large insects before they're eaten; or as a safety net for a newborn bat.

Life Upside Down

As almost everyone knows, bats like to hang upside down. It may be hard for us to imagine sleeping while hanging by our toes, but for bats, that's the most comfortable position there is. Their toes have sharp, curved claws that give a sure grip on a branch or cave wall.

In addition to napping, bats clean themselves, play or fight with one another, and some even give birth while hanging head-down. Bats frequently do turn themselves head-up and hang by their thumbs when they are excreting to keep from soiling themselves. Then they usually flip right back so that they can hang comfortably by their toes again.

For bats, the upside-down life seems to be a healthy one. They have an amazingly long life for animals of their size. Bats can live for twenty years or even longer! That may not seem so long compared with people, but for such a small animal, it is remarkable. Mice and similar-sized animals live only two to three years.

More to Come

You probably already know much more about bats than you did when you began this book. As you read on, you'll learn even more. For scientists who study bats, there are enough mysteries left to last many lifetimes.

According to one of the leading bat experts in the world, Merlin D. Tuttle, only about ten percent of bat species have been studied. And many questions remain even about some of the most common bats. Bats cannot be easily followed on their nightly trips. Some spend their days in unknown roosting places. Some spend their winters in undiscovered caves.

To understand more about bats, we'll look at the two major groups that scientists divide them into: *microchiroptera* (microbats, or small bats) and *megachiroptera* (megabats, or big bats). The names don't make sense in every case—there are some microbats that are larger than the smallest megabats. But there are important general traits that separate the two groups. In the following chapters you'll get a closer look at all kinds of bats. And you'll find out how and why they make their nightly journeys through the world of darkness.

3

Microbats

You climb into bed on a warm summer night. You're very sleepy. Just as your eyes start to close, you think you see something swoop through the air.

"No," you say to yourself, "just my imagination," and you go to sleep. But the next morning, as you rub your eyes and stretch, you notice a dark form hanging on the curtain. It looks like a small brown rag pinned to a fold of the material.

You cross the room to get a better look. That's no rag—it's a bat!

What should you do? Run? Call the fire department? Check your neck for bite marks?

The answers are no, no, and definitely no! Don't run out of the room. Don't bother the fire department. And don't expect to find teethmarks on your neck! (None of the bats that drink blood live in North America. And even those that do drink blood *don't* bite people's necks!)

The bat on your curtain is probably a young

22

animal that has taken a wrong turn. When it wakes up, it will want to escape even more than you want it to leave. Make it easy for the bat by following these steps: Close off the room. That will keep it from flying into other parts of your home. Then open the windows and screens and wait until the bat wakes up and finds its way out. (You'll find more ideas for getting bats out of your house later in this book.)

Even if you've never found a bat on your bed-room curtain, the chances are, no matter where you live, there are microbats living nearby. There are nearly 800 species of microbats living all over the world. About forty-two different types live in North America—and all North American bats are micros. Some species roost in the attics or under the eaves of buildings where people live or work. Others choose trees in city parks or along highways or rivers. Some take their day-time sleep under bridges or trestles or in garages or sheds. And some take shelter in caves and rock formations.

As their name tells you, the microbats are the small ones. In fact, the smallest known mammal is a microbat: the bumblebee bat of Thailand. It is small enough to sit in a teaspoon and weighs less than a penny. But there are microbats that weigh as much as eight ounces—about as much as four eggs. Most of the North American bats weigh between ¼ ounce and one ounce (that's between five and twenty large jelly beans), and they have a head and body that measure from 1½ to three inches in length.

Microbats, and megabats, too, are furry, with naked wings. The color of their fur may range from light tan, gray, or red to brown, black, or mottled. They can also have stripes on their faces or bodies. The real variety in their looks, however, comes from their faces and ears.

Their noses may be neat and rounded, long and pointed, plain or split, or have pieces of flesh shaped like spears, hearts, or horseshoes attached. They may have folds of skin on their chins, flaps on their lips, or wrinkles from forehead to mouth. Their ears may be small and rounded, long and pointed, wide or thin, furry or naked, black, tan, or even pink.

Bats may appear strange or frightening to us, but that's because we're not used to them. If you had never seen a hippopotamus and one appeared in your backyard, you'd probably think it looked strange and frightening, too! There is a reason bats look the way they do. The varied shapes, the nose-spears, the folds and flaps that may seem odd to us are part of the special equipment that makes the microbat a superstar of night hunting.

Hunting in the Dark

If you've ever tried grabbing mosquitoes out of the air, you know how hard they can be to

The Mexican long-nosed bat feeds on nectar from flowers.

A young Gambian epauleted bat.

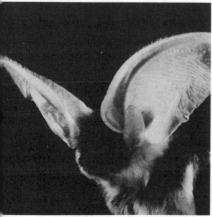

The very rare spotted bat lives in hot, dry sections of the southwestern United States.

The mastiff bat is not often seen because it roosts and feeds along high cliffs.

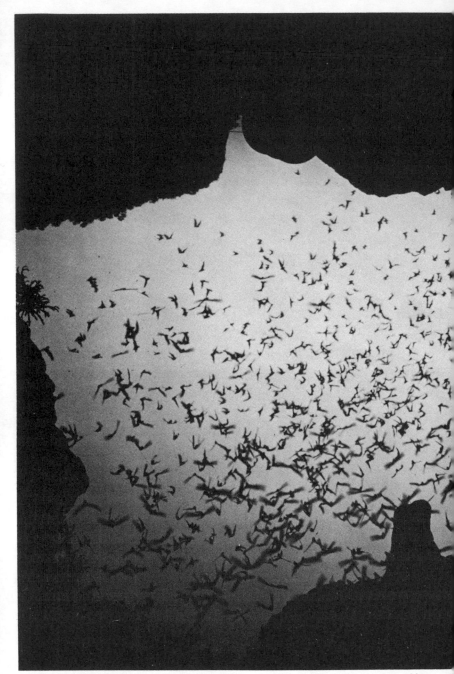

Bats fill the evening sky. Scenes like this were common in the past, before large numbers of bats were destroyed by man.

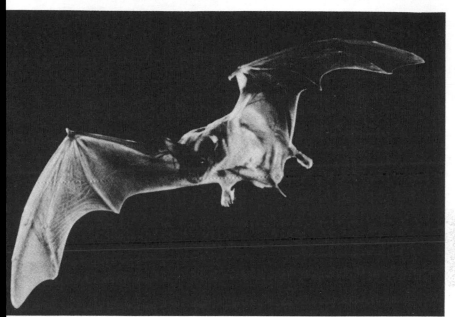

th the right tail winds, the Mexican free-tailed bat can fly up to sixty miles per hour, faster than
legal speed limit on many highways.

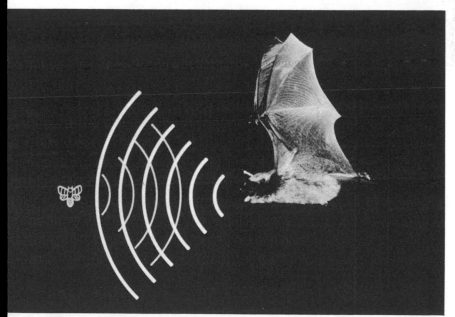

nks to echolocation, bats such as this little brown bat can hunt at night and find objects
ine as a single human hair.

In West Africa, these straw-colored flying fox bats gather in huge breeding colonies, up to one million at a time.

A small colony of big brown bats perches along wooden rafters. This is one of the most common species in the United States.

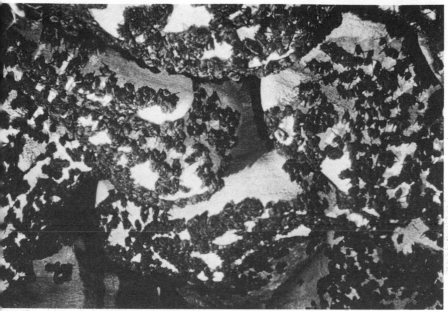

This colony of gray bats is hibernating in a stone cave. As a species, gray bats are struggling to survive. Twenty years ago there were five times as many as there are today.

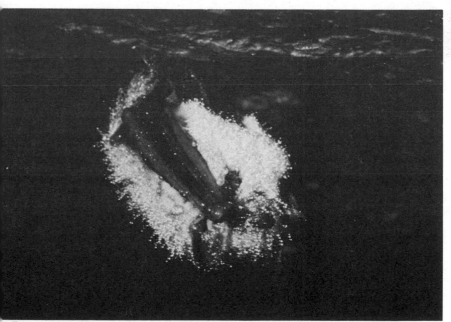

The Eastern pipistrelle is hibernating. The air in the cave where it is hanging is very moist. The moisture has collected in droplets on the bat's fur.

The D'Orbigny's round-eared bat has caught a large grasshopper. This particular bat was found in a rain forest in Panama.

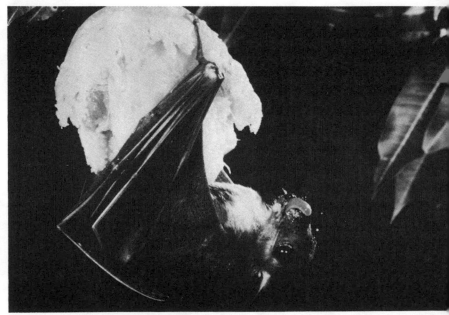

A very ripe mango is being eaten by an Egyptian fruit bat.

These are Gambian epauleted bats, a mother and her single pup. They are a fruit-eating species. The young bat learns which fruit to eat by licking the mother's mouth.

The wing of the flying fox includes a hand—with long, webbed fingers and a free thumb that points forward.

A vampire bat lands near its prey and then walks or hops closer.

catch. Now imagine trying to catch one mosquito every ten seconds and keeping up the pace for an hour. Now try doing it in the dark!

Impossible? Not if you're a *Myotis lucifugus*! That's the scientific name for the little brown bat, an animal that can be found throughout much of Canada and the United States. Like most microbats, it likes to eat insects best.

The little brown bat is especially fond of mosquitoes. Like the other insect-eaters, it is able to dart and swoop, moving quickly while making sudden changes in direction. It needs to be fast and precise, and it is. But flying skill alone does not explain how the little brown bat catches so many insects in the dark. How can it see what it's doing?

For years, people wondered about this. Part of the answer was uncovered in Italy at the end of the 1700s by a nature scientist named Lazzaro Spallanzani. It all began with an owl. Spallanzani knew that owls hunted at night. But he found that, in a completely dark room, an owl cannot find its way. It needs a tiny bit of light to see. When he set bats free in the same dark room, they flew around with no trouble. Even when he hung fine threads across the room, the bats never flew into them. What about bats that were actually blind? Spallanzani released a few blind animals. They were able to fly and feed without a problem.

Finally he tried plugging the ears of some bats.

These animals couldn't find their way. Somehow, he reasoned, bats needed to be able to hear in order to "see" in the dark.

It wasn't until 1938 that proof for Spallanzani's theory about bats could finally be found. A man named Donald Griffin who was studying at Harvard University was especially interested in bats. He knew a physics professor who was studying sounds that are pitched too high for humans to hear. The professor had a machine that could detect these sounds, called *ultrasonics*. Griffin brought some bats to the physics laboratory. When the machine was on, it showed that the room, which seemed silent, was actually filled with sound.

Human ears can usually pick up sounds that vibrate up to 20,000 times a second. But bats can make and hear sounds that vibrate up to 200,000 times a second! When bats are hunting in the dark, they send out high-pitched signals. When these signals strike an object, they bounce back, or echo. From these echoes, a bat can tell both the direction and speed of an insect.

This system of using sound and echo to track something is called *echolocation*. Using echolocation, bats can detect threads as fine as a hair. Except for one kind of megabat, only microbats echolocate. A micro uses its *larynx* or "voice box" to make the sounds that allow it to echolocate. (You'll learn about how a megabat echolocates later in this book.)

Just as you would have a hard time shouting to a friend across the street with your mouth shut, bats can't "shout" to their dinner with their mouths closed. Many types of microbat must fly with their mouths open in order to echolocate. That's one reason bats look so fierce: They fly throught the night, mouths open wide, their teeth showing. They may look as if they're ready to bite, but they're actually trying to make themselves heard!

Some bats can use their noses to broadcast sounds. That way, they can carry an insect in their mouths and hunt for more at the same time.

The fishing bulldog bat of Mexico, and Central and South America can store pieces of fish in pouches in its cheeks as it flies above the water looking for more to eat. It is one of several kinds of bats that head for open waters when they're hungry.

Scientists knew that the fishing bat used echolocation to help find its food. But that raised a question different from the questions about insect-eating bats. Sound waves travel poorly through water; how could a bat use sound and echo to find fish that were beneath the water?

Laboratory experiments helped find the answer. The bat could not find fish on wires that were held just beneath the water. But when tiny bits of wire were allowed to rise above the surface of the water, the bat found the fish just below the wire. Scientists reasoned that the bat was using echolocation to detect the small ripples in the water that fish make when they're near the surface.

When it has located its prey, the fishing bulldog bat swoops down, spears the fish with its large, sharp claws, and flies off. As it flies, looking for more food, it chops the fish into smaller pieces and stores the pieces in its mouth until it is ready to eat.

When scientists first learned of echolocation, they got an important clue about why some microbats look so strange. The nose leaves, spears, fleshy folds and horseshoe shapes all help direct the sounds that the bats send out. And the oversized ears help funnel the echoes back to the bat. Their ears may not be beautiful—but they're very effective when it comes to catching bugs and other food!

Microbats and Their Habits

It's not surprising that a group with so many different types of faces would have different habits as well. Most microbats eat insects, but not all. You've just read about a microbat that eats fish. There are also some that eat the nectar in flowers. The lesser long-nosed bat is one of them. It has a long nose, just as you might guess, and a long tongue, too, that looks almost like a toothbrush at the end. These are the perfect tools for an animal that likes to poke its snout into flowers and lap up the nectar inside. This bat is light enough to rest on a flower or hover in front of it, like a hummingbird, while it feeds.

As it pokes its head into a flower, the bat picks up a dusting of pollen on its face. Then when it moves to another flower to feed, some of the pollen is left behind. In that way, the animal serves the flowers that feed it by *pollinating* them, helping the plant to reproduce. This bat spends its summers in Arizona and New Mexico. In the fall it heads south to Mexico.

Even though most microbats eat insects, they don't all like the same insects. Their roosting habits vary as well. The little brown bat likes the insects that breed and live near water. So it often roosts in buildings that are close to rivers, lakes, or marshes. This bat is the one most likely to live near or in people's homes.

The big brown bat is found throughout North and Central America. It searches for insects in country fields, among the shady lanes of towns and villages, and even in big cities. It sometimes feasts on the insects that are attracted to street lights.

The Mexican free-tailed bat is a very sociable type. It lives in the American south and southwest and in Central America. These bats roost in huge colonies. Approximately 20,000,000 free-tailed bats live in Bracken Cave in Texas. Another 750,000 or so spend their summers roosting under a single bridge in Austin, Texas. Their favorite food is moths, and they eat tons of them. The Bracken Cave bats alone eat up to 250,000 pounds of insects every night!

Coping with Winter

Most of the nearly 800 types of microbats live in the tropics. Temperatures there are high year-round, and there are always plenty of insects. For the bats that live in North America, life is more complicated. There are big temperature changes from one season to the next, and the food supply falls off sharply in winter. (Just think of how many mosquitoes you see in the dead of winter. That gives you an idea of the problem facing a hungry bat.)

There are really only two ways these bats can keep from starving during the cold months: They can *migrate,* or move, to a warmer place; or they can stop eating by going into a long, deep sleep, known as *hibernation.* Some micros do one or the other and some do both, migrating to their hibernation sites.

Some of these bats that migrate travel many hundreds of miles to get to warmer regions. They may travel in the company of other types of bats or with migrating birds. Amazingly, bats seem to know exactly where they want to go to spend the winter. They return to the same winter homes—usually caves— year after year. And then they find their way back to their old summer homes when the seasons change again.

No one knows exactly how a bat can find its way over such long distances. They may use landmarks, such as mountain ranges and rivers, to help them stay on course. But experts think they may actually *memorize* the route, down to very small details.

Some migrating micros, like the Mexican free-tailed bats of Texas, do not hibernate at all. They spend their winters in Mexico or Central America where the warm temperatures mean a steady supply of insects. But more often, North American microbats do hibernate after first migrating to find the right spot.

Why don't they just stay put for the winter and sleep in the same roost where they lived all summer? They can't. Hibernation is not simply a matter of going to sleep. The temperature and the amount of moisture in the air have to be just right before a bat can hibernate. Only certain caves are "just right."

When it hibernates, a bat allows its body temperature to fall to the temperature of the air. So, a freezing air temperature would mean a freezing body temperature. If a bat's body temperature drops too low, ice crystals form in its blood, and it dies. For that reason, bats seek the exact conditions they need to hibernate safely. Many head for caves or mines where the temperature is cool but does not drop below the danger point.

Once it has reached the ideal spot, a bat begins the hibernation process by letting its body temperature drop. Our bodies must keep a constant temperature that is close to 98.6 degrees Fahrenheit. It's not possible for us to change our body temperature when we want to. If our temperature changes, rising with a very high fever or dropping to a dangerous chill, it's because we are sick.

Hibernating bats are different. They do not keep a constant body temperature. When they are active, their temperatures get very high, and when they are at rest, their temperatures fall. Their *metabolisms* also speed up or slow down according to their body temperatures. (Metabolism is the rate that an animal uses the energy it gets from food.)

After a bat's body temperature drops way down, it breathes very slowly. Its heartbeat, which can race along at thirteen beats a second when the bat is active, slows almost to a standstill—around fifteen to twenty beats a minute. It uses very little energy. For that reason, it can do without eating or drinking for long periods. This state of deep sleep and no activity is called *torpor.*

When the bat feels the need—and especially, when it is disturbed—it can come out of its torpid state. To do this, it warms itself up. Within minutes, its heartbeat and breathing return to active levels.

Bats may warm up and wake up several times during their months of hibernation. If the temperature in the cave changes, they may move to a new spot. If a warm spell brings a sudden rise in the insect supply, they may have a mid-winter snack. Then they cool off again and go back to sleep.

"Turning up the heat," however, uses a lot of energy. Each time a hibernating bat warms up and awakens, it uses some of the fat that it stored for the winter months—sometimes as much as thirty days' worth of fat. This can be a big problem for bats that hibernate in caves where people like to go exploring. Every time a visitor disturbs a hibernating bat, the animal will warm itself up. If this happens too often, the bat will use up its fat supply before the warm weather returns. It will have nothing to live off while it waits for the insect supply to build again, and it will starve.

Unfortunately for the bats, this does happen, all too often. According to Dr. Tuttle, all of the bats that are listed as endangered in the continental United States live in caves for at least part of the year. When people enter the caves at the wrong time, it can threaten the lives of thousands or even millions of bats. (Sadly, another reason cave bats are in trouble is that they're so easy to kill. One person can wipe out thousands of bats very quickly.)

A New Year Brings Babies

For bats that pass the winter in good health, the spring means the beginning of a new life cycle. At some point before or during the hibernating period, many microbats mate. But the baby bat does not develop until much later. This delay in the growth of the baby is important. It means that the females don't give birth during hibernation. If they did, there would not be enough food for the mothers and their newborn.

When the females come out of hibernation, they are thin and in need of food. Many fly off to "nursery colonies," where they live until it is time for their babies to be born. These colonies are in a place where the temperature is high and there is a big supply of insects. Most bats return to the same colonies year after year.

Being a newborn bat isn't always easy. For the tiny bats, getting a good toehold can be a matter of life and death.

Baby bats are born while their mothers dangle upside down from the ceiling of a cave or an attic beam. Depending on the kind of bat it is, the mother may catch her baby in the "hammock" formed by her tail membrane. Then the baby crawls across the mother in search of a nipple. When it finds one, it latches on.

At birth, bat babies are usually furless and blind. Many are born with special teeth called *milk teeth*. They use these teeth to hold on to their mothers while they feed. They are also born with oversized feet and claws, which help them to hang in the roost on their own whenever their mothers go out in search of food.

Whether they're hanging on to mother or dangling from a cave ceiling, the tiny bats never really stop holding on to *something* from the moment of birth. A baby that loses its grip and falls will almost certainly die. Most bats do not seem able to help their fallen infants.

Within a few days of birth, the bats will be able to see. After a while, they'll be wrapped in a coat of new-grown fur. And soon their wings will be strong enough for flight. Before long, within about five weeks, they will be independent and ready to hunt for food by themselves.

4

Vampire Bats

Shhh! Something's moving in the grave-yard. Shadows shift across a moonlit path. A face appears, deathly white above a black cape. Piercing eyes stare out. Sharpened teeth glint in the eerie light.

It's a vampire—the horrible creature that stalks the night, searching for human victims. It wants to drink their blood. But it will return to the graveyard before dawn. There it will sleep away the daylight hours until its next night of horror....

Tales like this have haunted people's dreams for centuries. There is no shortage of legends about blood-sucking vampires! So, when Europeans first learned of a blood-drinking bat, they named it "vampire."

The reputation for being scary and dangerous stuck to the bat, along with the name. That's because most people didn't like bats much to begin with.

The Real Thing

The facts about vampire bats are a lot less frightening than the stories. Vampires are rare. There are only three kinds of vampire bat out of almost 1,000 kinds of bat worldwide. All vampire bats are found in Mexico, and Central and South America. The most famous one, the common vampire bat, is a small, shy animal covered with reddish brown or gray-brown fur. Its head and body are about three inches long and it weighs a little more than an ounce—about the same as a small bag of potato chips. It has a small, pushed-in snout; short, pointed ears; and a notch in its lower lip. It also has long, triangular-shaped incisor teeth and very long thumbs that help in its unique ability to walk.

The common vampire most often preys on large hoofed animals, such as cattle and horses. Sometimes it will attack goats or pigs. It rarely attacks people, but if it does, it usually bites the big toe! The two other types of vampire seem to prefer birds.

Although vampires are able to echolocate, they probably don't need to when they are hunting large prey. Vampires seem to use sight and smell to help them find their way.

When it has located its target, the bat flies up to the sleeping animal and lands silently, often on an animal's back. Sometimes it lands a few feet away and creeps over to the animal. Then it neatly slices off a small piece of skin using its razor-sharp teeth. The cut is quick and painless. The sleeping victim usually isn't aware of what's going on. (Even people who are bitten by vampires generally don't realize it until morning when they notice the blood.)

There is a special chemical in a vampire's saliva that stops blood from clotting. For that reason, the wound keeps bleeding while the bat feeds. Vampire bats don't actually suck blood. They curl their tongues into a tube like a straw. They hold the "tongue-tube" with its open side downward against the notch in their lower lips. Then they lap the blood into their mouths through the "tube." Only about a tablespoon of blood is needed to make a meal for a vampire bat. Most animals can easily give up that much blood without harm. If, however, many vampires feed on the same animal in a single night, or if they return to the same animals night after night, the blood loss to the victim is much greater.

Vampires feed in and around animals that are much larger than they are—sometimes *thousands* of times larger! So they may have to move fast to get out of the way of a kicking leg or swishing tail. As it happens, vampires are very quick and graceful. Unlike any other kind of bat, they can stroll along, walking almost upright on their legs. At other times, they lean forward on their wrists or thumbs. They can run or leap, hop forward or backward, or just scamper away. If there were an award for best gymnast in the bat world, the vampire would be the winner.

Their skill at walking, crawling, and jumping also comes in handy when they roost. Vampires, like most bats, favor narrow, hidden cracks in caves or creases in rocks or trees. In order to move into position in their roosts, they often have to scramble along steep or narrow passages.

Vampires have another surprising trait—they sometimes help out other bats in need. Vampires have been known to adopt an orphan bat or give aid and food to other vampires that need it. This behavior is rare in many animals. According to Dr. Tuttle, they have many of the type of qualities that we expect to find in good, kind people.

The greatest damage done by vampire bats is thought to be the spread of rabies. Rabies is a fatal disease caused by a virus. Any mammal, including humans, can get rabies. It is passed on in the saliva of an infected animal, usually by a bite. An animal that catches rabies will usually not live very long.

For years, it was thought that bats could get rabies *without* getting sick themselves. If that were true, the bats could live for years infecting others and spreading rabies until it was out of control. Vampires with rabies would be especially dangerous since they bite animals as part of their normal behavior.

Scientists now know that bats cannot pass on rabies without becoming sick themselves. A bat with rabies—like a dog or a raccoon with rabies—will soon die. They do not seem to go through a "furious" stage, becoming wild and violent as other animals do, but a sick bat will often act differently than a healthy one. It might flop on the ground, unable to fly, for instance. For this reason, it is *never* a good idea to pick up a bat. Any bat that will let you catch it could be sick.

Even though vampire bats do become sick and die from rabies, they can still be a problem, especially for cattle ranchers. A sick vampire that is not yet too sick to fly can bite and infect its victim. Health experts have developed ways to protect livestock from rabid bats.

False Vampires

When the Australian giant false vampire was first spotted, people thought it was a vampire bat. It does not drink blood, but it is a carnivorous, or flesh-eating bat. In addition to eating some large insects it also hunts for small animals including some kinds of small bats.

The Australian bat may have a wingspan of more than two feet. It is the largest of a group of false vampires that live in the Old World tropics (Australia, parts of Africa and Asia, and many of the Pacific islands). The largest bat in the New World (North and South America) is another wrongly named creature: Linne's false vampire. It is about the same size as the Australian bat and eats small animals, fruit, and insects.

Vampire bats prefer cattle blood and, generally, only bite people when they can't find their preferred food. But in areas where real vampire bats roost, it's probably not a good idea for people to sleep out in the open where they might look too much like dinner to a hungry vampire. As for people living among false vampire bats, the only thing to fear from vampires is bad dreams!

5

Megabats

If you were writing a horror movie about a gigantic flying monster, you might want to call it *"Megabat!"* The star of your film could be a huge bat with a hundred-foot wingspan and claws the size of steam shovels. In the movie, the bat might carry off a bus full of screaming people, or it might break a skyscraper in half with one of its giant wings.

The real megabats, or megachiroptera, would never make it as horror movie stars. They're only big when you compare them with the microbats. And even then, there are exceptions. A megabat called the southern blossom bat is much smaller than many of the micros!

The wingspans of megabats range from about ten inches to almost six feet. The smallest megas, like the southern blossom, weigh only about half an ounce—as much as five Ping-Pong balls. The giants of the group reach a weight of twenty golf balls. That's about two pounds.

Megabats are also known as fruit bats since they usually eat only fruit, flowers, nectar, and pollen. They can also go by the name "flying fox," and it's easy to see where the name comes from. Many fruit bats have fox-like or dog-like faces, with big eyes and pointed ears. Their fur may be gray, reddish brown, dark brown, or tan. Unlike the microbats, which make their homes in all parts of the world, megabats live only in the Old World tropics. Flowers and fruit grow in the tropics year round. As a result, the bats have a steady supply of food. They don't need to hibernate as other bats do.

Megabats and Their Habits

Most fruit bats roost out in the open, hanging from branches in colonies called *camps*. Some make their homes in treetops high above the traffic of large towns. They dangle, like heavy, ripe pieces of fruit, spaced out along the branches.

On very hot days, they may be seen fanning themselves with their wings. When the weather turns rainy, the bats can wrap their wings around themselves, as if they were shut up inside a closed umbrella. The wings protect them against the cold as well.

All bats make a lot of noise. When microbats sound off, it's usually too high-pitched for our ears. But the racket made by flying foxes is in a pitch that people hear very well. These bats screech, scream, and flutter their wings. They fight over the best spot to roost or the branch with the ripest fruit. They are also noisy eaters. They bite hungrily into their juicy food, swallowing the sweet liquid and spitting out the pulp and seeds.

Their favorite foods are sweet and ripe: mangoes, avocadoes, bananas, figs, guavas, and peaches. Since fruit bats often carry a fruit away to eat it, they help spread the seeds that will grow into new plants. And many fruits have developed in a way that is ideal for attracting bats: They hang on long stems. They give off a strong scent. And they stay on the tree until they're very ripe and easily picked.

Many flowers are especially well suited to the bats that feed on nectar and pollen. These flowers blossom at night. The flowers that attract bats are usually greenish white, red, brown, or dark blue in color. They are usually large and easy to get to. Some have long stems, and some grow right out of a tree trunk. "Bat flowers" also have a special aroma. Some smell musky, others smell like overripe fruit.

After raiding a flower for its nectar and pollen, a megabat flies to the next blossom to feed. In the process, it carries pollen on its fur from one flower to the next, just as the microbat does. This makes it possible for the flower to reproduce. The bat flowers depend on bats for pollination just as the bats depend on the flowers for food.

As you read earlier, the insect-eating microbats use echolocation to help them hunt. But with one exception (described later in this chapter), megabats do not echolocate. They can't and they don't have to. Their dinner doesn't run away! It stays still on a tree or stem, waiting to be eaten. The fruit bats can use their eyes and noses to find the fruit or flowers they need.

Nocturnal animals that need to see in the dark usually have one trait in common—large eyes. The larger the surface of the eye, the more light can enter. Fruit bats have large eyes that are perfect for looking around at night. Even in the very dimmest light they can make out sharp images. They cannot see color very well, but with their sense of smell, they can find their way to their favorite foods.

From a human point of view, the large eyes of the fruit bats make them seem more friendly than their microbat cousins. And since most fruit bats don't echolocate, they have evolved without the spears, leaves, wrinkles, and flaps that make many microbats look so unusual. Even people who shudder when someone mentions "bat," might want to scratch the ear of a fruit bat.

In Australia, some people have adopted injured fruit bats, or flying foxes, feeding and sheltering them until they are able to care for themselves. These people report that the animals check in at their old homes from time to time. Some of the bats even bring their new babies for a visit!

Clearly, megabats in the tropics have a much different reputation from the microbats that live in temperate areas like the United States and Europe. Perhaps the final proof of this is that megabats are a favorite food among many Pacific islanders. Of course, being too well liked can be as dangerous as being disliked. Flying foxes on the island of Guam have been overhunted for their meat. One type of bat has already been killed off and another is in danger of becoming extinct.

Bat expert Dr. Merlin Tuttle has worked with leaders on another island, American Samoa, to protect bats there from suffering the same fate. New laws put limits on bat hunting, and a national park was established in 1988 to make sure that there will be more bats for generations to come.

Mega Babies

As you learned earlier, many microbats mate before the cold weather comes and they begin to hibernate, but their babies develop and are born in the warmer weather. For the megabats living in the tropics, the seasons are much less extreme and there is food year-round. They don't hibernate. So for most megas, as soon as they mate, the babies begin to develop inside the mother.

Megabats, like micros, usually give birth to one baby at a time. And most megas mate only once a year. After the baby is born, it may spend its time hidden under its mother's wing. Since many of the fruit bats roost in trees out in the open, the mother's wing is a shield against wind, rain, and sun.

In fact, unlike the insect-eating micros, many mega mothers take their new babies along for the ride on the nightly feeding trips. Because the megas tend to be larger than the micros, they are able to fly with the added weight of their off-spring. And if carrying a heavy baby makes them fly a little less skillfully, it's not as important as it would be for an insect-eating bat. After all, the micros have to dart and swoop to catch their flying food. But fruit bats can just head for a handy fruit tree and land squarely on their meal. They don't have to be precise flyers in order to be well fed.

During the day, as it hangs from tree branches, a young megabat may wander away from its mother. If that happens, the mother and baby can find each other by calling out and using their sense of smell.

Using Sound to "See"

Many types of megabats have a very small range; they may be found only in a small section of the Old World Tropics, on a single island, or in a narrow strip along one edge of a continent.

The rousette bats are different. They are found in a variety of places. And unlike most megabats, the rousettes live in caves, tombs, and other dark shelters.

What really sets the rousette bats apart is their echolocation. The rousettes can use their sound system to "see" in the dark. That is how they are able to live in places too dark for most other megabats. In fact, they seem to use their echolocation only when they are in dark roosts. When they come out of their roosts, they turn off the echolocation before they begin to hunt for food. Then they rely on their eyesight and keen sense of smell like other megabats.

Echolocation for rousette bats starts in the mouth. They use their tongues to make clicking sounds. (These sounds are easily heard by the human ear.) This is different from the echolocation of the microbats. As you learned earlier, when a micro echolocates, it emits a high-pitched sound that comes from its larynx, or voice box, rather than from its tongue. For that reason, micros have much more control over the sounds they make than the rousettes do. Using their tongue clicks, rousettes cannot "see" as far or make out as many details as the micros can with their echolocation. But they don't have to rely as heavily on their echolocation as the micros do.

6

Bats in Your Life

Imagine for a moment that all the bats have disappeared. A quarter of the world's mammals are gone. What does that mean to you?

In the first place, it means you'll be seeing a lot more insects. Without the bats to gobble them up, there will be *millions* of pounds more insects each year—biting insects; crop-eating insects; insects of all kinds. That's a lot of ruined picnics!

All those extra bugs will probably mean a lot more chemicals in your life. Insect-eating bats are natural bug killers—and safe for the environment! Without them, people would have to spray and dust their farms and gardens with chemicals to fight the growing bug population. Those chemicals cost money and often make people sick. (And bats do a much better job than any chemical could!)

The world will miss the fruit- and nectar-eating bats, as well. Without them, many important wild plants will become extinct. As bats feed, they spread seeds and help pollinate the plants they visit. Everyone knows how important bees are in pollinating plants. But very few people realize how many plants depend on bats to help them reproduce and grow.

Without bats, there will be no wild peaches, dates, bananas, carob, mangoes, figs, avocados, balsa wood, cashews, cloves, or kapok, which is used in making bandages and life preservers. In some countries, the loss of bats will mean the end of millions of dollars' worth of timber and fruit. Bats help hundreds of different types of plants to grow. And many of them are important to people.

Bats are useful in other ways:

*Bat droppings that pile up in caves, known as *guano,* are used as a fertilizer and in many important scientific studies.

*Droppings from cave bats also serve as *nutrients*, the basis for many other forms of cave life.

*With what they have learned from studying bats, scientists have found ways to help blind people to get around on their own.

*Research on vampire bats may lead to a safe blood-thinner that will help people who have had heart attacks and strokes.

*Scientists study how bats hear to get clues to the way human ears work.

Perhaps most importantly, people can learn from bats that all life is important. Even an animal that looks or acts strangely should be respected. Like bats, such an animal may be a key part of the chain of life on earth.

If you live in North America, it may be hard to imagine why a rain forest is important to you.

But without the chain of plants and animals which live in the rain forests, our own futures are in great danger. We need rain forests to make sure we will always have enough water, oxygen, and other essential materials to sustain life.

Bats spread many of the seeds that lead to the growth of new areas of rain forest. That makes the connection between people and bats very clear. They are as important to our future as we are to theirs.

Living Peacefully with Bats

What can you do for bats?

The first thing is to learn about them. (Reading this book is a great way to start.) The more you know about bats, the more there is to like about them. And the less there is to fear! You can tell others about what you know about bats, too. Most of the bad things that people think about bats are not even true.

If you have a "bat encounter," be calm and smart. If you see a bat outdoors, on the ground, don't touch it—it may be sick. A normal, healthy bat would not let you catch it while it's awake. If it's in a place where other people might pass by it, tell an adult. You might call an animal shelter.

What about that bat we met earlier—the one that was hanging from your bedroom curtains? You can leave the windows open and wait until it awakens and flies away. Or you can ask an adult to catch it while it is sleeping.

To catch a roosting bat, cover it gently with an empty coffee can or box. Carefully slide a piece of firm cardboard under the bat to trap it and keep it in the container. Then take it outdoors. Wait five minutes before uncovering it so that the bat will be fully awake and ready to fly.

Never touch a bat with bare hands. Most likely it is a healthy animal that cannot give you any disease. But it is probably very frightened of you. It could try to bite in self-defense. If someone has to touch the bat, an adult wearing thick leather work gloves should do it.

If you want to offer a welcome to bats—and help cut down on neighborhood insects, you might want to put up a bat house. A bat house is a little like a bird house, but without the floor. You can get plans and instructions for building a shelter for bats by writing to: Bat Conservation International, Inc., P.O. Box 162603, Austin, Texas 78716-2603.

If a colony of bats has already moved into *your* house, don't panic. Without hurting them, you can "lock" the bats out of your house by using netting. The U.S. Fish and Wildlife Service, your state wildlife service, or Bat Conservation International can tell you what to do.

Now that you have the facts about bats, you know there's one less night creature to fear. If you ever come face-to-face with a bat, you can see the animal for what it is: valuable, gentle, fascinating...an important part of our world.